The Complete Guide to House Sitting

Nik Rivers

ISBN-13: 978-1535003155

ISBN-10: 1535003154

www.hjpublishing.com

About this book

A few years ago, house sitting was relatively unheard of. Only a small group of travel-lovers and an even smaller group of homeowners knew about it. These days it's a regular talking point everywhere: from travel blogs and pet forums to major newspapers, travel magazines and TV shows.

It's not surprising that house sitting has become so popular so quickly. House sitting is an attractive concept for both homeowners and potential sitters. Homeowners can relax with the knowledge that their home and pets are being cared for while they travel. House sitters get free accommodation in return for feeding the cat, walking the dog and making sure the property is ticking over smoothly. It's win-win for both parties and neither one has to pay the other a dime.

This new popularity means there are more house sits to choose from now than ever before. Every month thousands of new house sitting opportunities become available. There are plenty to choose from in Australia, the USA and the UK. Every now and then house sits crop up in more exotic locations such as Kenya, the Caribbean, and Japan. These opportunities can be snapped up by eager house sitters: many of whom go from one house sit to another, slowly making their way around the world and paying only their food and transport costs.

Of course, this also means that more people than ever before want to try their hand at house sitting. Newcomers find themselves competing against a huge number of other house sitters. Many boast years of experience and have plenty of glowing references from previous clients. Naturally, homeowners tend to pick people with experience. It's understandable: imagine what you would do if you were trying to decide which complete stranger should look after your home.

As a new house sitter with little (if any) experience it can be difficult to get accepted for house sits. Homeowners want experienced house sitters but it's impossible to get that experience without someone first throwing you a rope and letting you house sit for them. This Catch-22 situation is a stumbling block for almost every new house sitter, causing many to simply give up before they even get started.

But it doesn't have to be that way! Having house sat all over the world, written extensively about house sitting for a number of major blogs, and interviewed countless house sitters, the team at housesittingguide.com know exactly what it takes to go far. We've put together all of our wisdom about house sitting, particularly about getting started, and now we're ready to share it with you.

Throughout this book we'll be looking at everything you need to know about house sitting: from finding opportunities to applying for house sits to tips on what you should do during the house sit itself to ensure you get invited back again.

We hope that after reading this book, you'll be able to follow in the footsteps of thousands of other travel lovers and that through house sitting you'll be able to enjoy the same cheap yet luxurious lifestyle we've come to enjoy ourselves.

Contents

Part 1: Getting Started

What is house sitting?

House sitting is looking after someone else's home (and usually their pets as well) while they're away. In return for looking after the property and pets you get to stay there for free.

Every house sit is different. The home you look after will be different from the previous one, as will the pets, the owners and the location as well. You could be house sitting an apartment in the center of New York one week and looking after a farmhouse in rural England the next.

Readers of housesittingguide.com have looked after a vast array of properties including:

- Renovated farmhouses in the French countryside

- A four-story mansion beside the beach in Thailand

- A property in a village in the English countryside

The world, or at least anywhere house sitting opportunities exist, is your oyster. Thanks to house sitting it's a very affordable oyster as well. With only your transportation (e.g. flights) and living costs (e.g. food and drink) to worry about, house sitting makes it possible to travel cheaply on both a short and long-term basis. There are many house sitters who've been doing this for several years; going from house sit to house sit and seeing the world on an incredibly small budget.

Although this book focuses on the benefits of house sitting from the house sitter's point of view, the house sitter isn't the only person to benefit. House sitting also benefits:

The homeowner who gets his property and pets looked after (for free).

The pets who get looked after in the familiar surroundings of their own home (instead of going to a kennel).

What's so great about house sitting?

The following are just some of the benefits that house sitting has to offer.

Live rent free

This needs no explanation. Accommodation is one of the biggest costs for any traveler, but when you house sit it's no longer a concern.

Stay in bigger, better properties

Space is a precious commodity when you're travelling, especially if you're travelling as a couple and even more so if you're travelling with kids. Sharing the same hotel room, tent or small apartment with other people can put a strain on any relationship.

Because house sitting involves staying in other people's homes, you'll mostly be staying in properties larger than the majority of hotel rooms and vacation rentals. You're also likely to have access to more mod cons: little luxuries like coffee machines and Wi-Fi or dishwashers and washing machines.

Save money by eating in

After flights and accommodation, food is the next major travel expense. This is especially true if you're staying in a hotel or a vacation rental that's so sparsely furnished that you're forced to dine out all the time.

Going out for dinner is fun, but it does lose its magic after a while. Particularly when it eats into your travel budget and expands your waistline. A good kitchen equipped with a selection of kitchen utensils and pots and pans can be expected in most house sits. You'll not only save money by eating at home but your meals will probably be healthier as well.

Live like a local

Because you'll be looking after someone else's home, you'll probably be staying in a part of town where locals live and not in the tourist district where the hotels are based. You might be a little further from the attractions, but it's worth it when you consider what you're getting in return.

Most homeowners are a treasure trove of useful information about the area and will be able to give you a good mix of both touristy and non-touristy things to see and do: as well as great tips on local markets and upcoming events.

It's fulfilling

Although house sitters do exceptionally well out of the house sitting arrangement (they get to live somewhere for free), homeowners benefit as well. They get to go away knowing that their home and pets are being properly looked after, rather than worrying about their pet being locked away in a kennel or that their house might be getting broken into.

Being able to offer this peace-of-mind to homeowners is incredibly fulfilling.

That trip of a lifetime is suddenly affordable

London, New York, Sydney, and the Caribbean - these are all expensive locations to visit but locations where house sits frequently pop up. Without the cost of accommodation to worry about, and the opportunity to save money by cooking at home, these dream trips are suddenly within anyone's grasp thanks to house sitting.

Make new, four-legged friends

Pet sitting is part of the 'job' but most house sitters find it actually ends up being the most rewarding part of the experience. Having dogs to walk and cats to cuddle is a lot of fun, and not something most people are able to do while travelling. After house sitting some of your best travel memories will include a pet or two in them.

Where can I house sit?

You can find house sits all over the world. But even though the odd opportunity will pop up in China or Mozambique, the bulk of opportunities tend to come from one of two places:

English-speaking countries

Even though house sitting is growing in popularity worldwide, the majority of people using these websites are English speakers. You'll see a lot of house sits in countries like Australia, New Zealand, the USA, Canada, the UK and Ireland. It may not sound very exotic, but these are generally some of the most expensive countries to travel in. These house sits are definitely worth their weight in gold.

Expat Hotspots

A huge percentage of people that search for house sitters online are English speaking expats. Popular countries like France, Spain, Italy and some parts of South-East Asia are all places with a high number of house sits. Most expats are retirees so the majority of house sits posted by them are in quieter, rural areas. It's much easier to find a house sit in the Dordogne than it is to find one in Paris.

Why do people get house sitters?

You may be wondering why people get house sitters in the first place. Why don't they just put their pets into boarding kennels or ask a neighbor to take care of them? It's a good question. To answer that, it's important to understand just how important pets are to the homeowners you'll come across while house sitting.

For 95% of these homeowners, pets are the reason they get a sitter. Having the lawns mowed, the pool cleaned, the plants watered and even protecting the home from burglars is secondary to knowing that their pets are being properly looked after. This doesn't just mean feeding and cleaning up after them: it means giving them the kind of one-on-one attention they would get if their owners were there. Many homeowners have said that they've cancelled vacations before because they weren't willing to put their pets into boarding kennels.

It's not for a lack of good boarding kennels. While there are a few bad boarding kennels and catteries out there, there are also plenty of good ones as well. It's just that as good as these kennels are, few are able to offer what a house sitter can and that's one-on-one care and

9

attention for the pet in the familiar surroundings of its own home.

Of course getting a house sitter, essentially having someone who's a complete stranger, look after your home and pets is a big deal to most homeowners. Nearly all pursue the neighbor or friend route first. But when the friend or neighbor is unable to do it, homeowners start thinking of other alternatives. It's usually at this point that they come across house sitting.

As the idea begins to take hold, homeowners start to see the other benefits of getting a house sitter. Home security is just one example. Just having someone living in the home is enough to deter most burglars. Then there's the benefit of having someone there in case anything goes wrong, for example if a pipe bursts. After that there are all the small benefits like having the plants watered, the pool cleaned and the mail taken in. When you put it all together, getting a house sitter makes a lot of sense for many homeowners.

Will I get paid to house sit?

This book focuses on house sitting for free in return for free accommodation. While there's nothing to stop you putting a price tag on your house sitting services, it's unlikely this will be a major earner for you given that you'll be competing against people who are offering the same service for free.

It is possible to set up a business where you house sit for others and charge for your services. Generally speaking though, these businesses tend to be local businesses. If you go down this route you'll probably only get clients within a couple of hour's drive of where you're based. Very few of the house sitting business out there are international businesses.

Although this book is more focused on the free, travel-focused side of house sitting and not about setting up a house sitting business, we have included a small chapter on house sitting for profit towards the end of this book.

Before we go any further

We've talked a lot about the pros of house sitting. Staying in other people's homes in exchange for minding their pets is a great way to see the world. Without the cost of accommodation to factor into your travel budget, you can travel for cheaper and for longer as well. House sitting definitely has its plus points.

But as great as house sitting is, it isn't always perfect and it certainly isn't always easy. Before setting yourself up as a house sitter, bear the following points in mind.

House sitting can be hard work

Most house sits mean a few hours of work a day, which can vary from feeding the cats and walking the dogs to cleaning the pool and mowing the lawn. At the end of the house sit you'll need to make sure the house is spotless for the homeowner's return. Depending on the size of the property this can take up to a whole day of cleaning: sometimes longer.

It's a lot of responsibility

Homeowners want someone who will be there to take care of things if and when they go wrong. If the cat gets sick, you'll need to take it to the vet. If a pipe bursts, you'll need to turn off the water and arrange for someone to come and fix it. If one of the pets goes missing, you'll need to find it.

Dealing with situations like these can be very stressful especially if you're doing it in another country and even more so if you're trying to do it all in another language.

You won't get paid to house sit

Not paying rent can save you a ton of money but if you plan to do this for longer than the length of a standard vacation you will need to have some kind of income to live on. Whether that's savings, a pension or income from a freelance job, make sure you have enough cash to cover your stay.

You'll need to be flexible about where you house sit

House sitting works best when you're flexible on both location and date. For example if you only want to house sit in San Francisco in September: you might find there are no house sits available or, if there are, you might not get picked for them.

But even if there aren't any house sits in San Francisco in September, there'll still be thousands of other house sits worldwide, and plenty in the USA. Be flexible. Focus on the dates you're available to house sit and where you can travel to easily. Then see which house sits you're interested in doing. Although there will be a few house sits in San Francisco, the majority will be in far less trendy locations, often towns and rural locations. Although having to be flexible is a downside of house sitting, the other side of that coin is that you will end up discovering lots of new places, places you probably never considered visiting before. Visiting, say, a small town in Spain, as opposed to visiting Barcelona, will give you a much better feel for the 'real Spain'.

House sitting can be competitive

When applying for a house sitting assignment, there could be anywhere from a handful to more than a hundred other people applying. The problem isn't so much the number of other sitters, although most homeowners don't tend to read past 30-40 applications so you do need to make sure you get your application in as soon as possible. The problem, at least for the apathetic house sitter, is the quality of the other house sitters. Some are just incredible and will go the extra mile at every available opportunity. Naturally, these are the house sitters homeowners tend to pick.

If you want to do well as a house sitter, and get picked for a lot of house sits, you'll need to be one of these house sitters as well.

House sitting is a lot of responsibility

As a house sitter you'll be looking after someone else's home, and ensuring that their home along with the possessions they have in it and their pets, are kept safe for the duration of the house sit. This is no small undertaking. Although it's very rare that something goes horribly wrong during a house sit, sometimes things do. Many house sitters have had pets go missing during a house sit and will tell you just how stressful this can be.

Of course, this doesn't happen on every house sit. In fact, it's the rarity. Regardless, you should always be aware of just how much responsibility you're taking on.

You'll be dealing with people (and people can be hard work)

Aside from needing a house sitter, there's no common feature that unites homeowners. They're all different. Some will be young, some will be old. Some will give you plenty of personal space during the handover, while others will expect you to be around them for most of the time that they're there. Some will be neat freaks, while others will be surprisingly untidy. For all of these extremes, there will also be all of the other homeowners that fall somewhere in the middle. In short, homeowners are a very diverse group of people.

Every new house sitting assignment means dealing with a new person, couple, or family. You probably won't know a lot about them: house sitting websites tend to focus on providing homeowners with a lot of information about sitters but rarely the other way round. Each new house sit (and the homeowners that come with it) brings its own collection of interpersonal challenges.

For the most part, homeowners are a wonderful bunch of people. Nearly all understand that house sitting is a two-way exchange. They'll want to make this work as much as you do, and if both of you accommodate each other, it will. Unfortunately, every now and then you'll come across a difficult homeowner. It's hard to spot these bad eggs in advance, although you will develop a better gut reaction the more house sits you do.

The house sitting application process can be frustrating

Every day, depending on how many house sitting sites you're a member of, tens to hundreds of new house sits will arrive in your inbox. Each of these opportunities deserves a somewhat (if not completely) unique application email which takes time and effort. Over time you'll get better at speeding up the process.

You'll put a lot of effort into each individual email but you won't always hear back from the homeowner. Some will be overwhelmed by the amount of applications they get and will ignore a lot of the messages. Others just won't consider what it's like to be on the other end of the application process. Others you'll hear back from and may even have a good deal of correspondence with but in the end they'll pick someone else.

Applying for house sits is hard work. It takes time and effort and it's frustrating when you don't land the job. The only way to deal with it is to not let it affect you personally and to just keep on applying for new opportunities.

Picking a house sitter is also hard work for homeowners. Often there's no obvious choice and several house sitters are all equally suitable. There can only be one house sitter and so homeowners will usually go with their gut (i.e. whoever they've made a connection with). Although it's not much consolation to the house sitters that don't get picked, it's often hard for the homeowner having to reject so many suitable applicants.

Understand that house sitting is a numbers game. Even the best house sitters don't get accepted for every house sit they apply for (although their ratio is certainly better than most). Experienced house sitters realize that house sitting is often just a case of throwing the net out and seeing what you get back in.

Part II: House Sitting Sites

An introduction to house sitting sites

You'll find the majority of house sits through house sitting websites. These sites connect people who need a house sitter and people who want to house sit.

There are several house sitting websites out there, with new ones starting up all of the time. Some of the sites we discuss in this book are new while others have been around for more than a decade. They range in quality and price, with the cheapest costing around $20 USD per year and the more expensive costing closer to $90 or $100 USD.

Regardless of whether it costs $20 or $90 to join a site, it only takes one house sit to make joining that site worthwhile. If the accommodation is nice and the house sit lasts for more than a couple of days you've definitely got your money's worth. Most house sits last for at least ten days if not longer. This usually translates to hundreds of dollars, and often thousands of dollars in accommodation savings.

How do house sitting sites work?

The following is an example of the typical house sitting process.

Alice, a homeowner in Los Angeles needs someone to look after her home and pets for two weeks while she is on vacation. She hears about house sitting from a friend and joins one of the many house sitting sites. There she posts an advert looking for a sitter with information about her pets, what responsibilities there will be and when she'll be away.

Meanwhile in London, John, one of the members of the house sitting site, sees the advert and decides this is a house sit he'd like to do. He writes a message to Alice, explaining why he would be a good fit.

Alice looks at John's message and his profile on the house sitting site and decides that he might be right for the job. She also has messages from a couple of other sitters which she reads through, making a shortlist of whoever else she thinks might be a good fit.

John and Alice email back and forth, asking each other questions.

Alice then arranges individual phone calls through Skype with John and the other candidates that she thinks are suitable.

Finally, Alice decides that John is the best fit and offers him the house sit. He accepts, naturally, and begins making plans to travel to Los Angeles.

Tip: Most house sitting sites offer two forms of e-mail alerts: daily roundups and real-time alerts. Daily roundup emails are a roundup of every house sitting assignment that has been posted that day. Real-time alerts mean you get an email as soon as the house sit has been posted on the site. Check your settings and make sure that you're signed up for the real-time email alerts, as this will ensure that you are able to apply for a house sit as soon as it is published. Many homeowners stop reading new applications after they receive 30-40 applications and this sometimes happens by the time it gets to the end of the day and the daily roundup emails go out.

House sitting websites (the main ones)

In this section we'll look at the main house sitting websites. These websites post house sitting opportunities from all over the world so, unless you're only interested in house sitting in one specific country, these are the sites you should consider signing up for. The following is a brief overview of each site. More information, including reviews from members of each of the sites, can be found at Housesittingguide.com

Trusted Housesitters

- Annual Fee: $99 USD

- Promo code: 'housesittingguide' (10% off new memberships)

- More Information & Reviews of Trusted Housesitters: www.housesittingguide.com/sites/trusted-housesitters/

Trusted Housesitters is the largest of the house sitting sites, posting 3-4 times as many house sits per month as the next biggest site. It's constantly being improved, with new features added every couple of months.

This is the most popular house sitting site and the one that most of the people interviewed at housesittingguide.com recommend. It's more expensive than most sites but as there are more house sitting opportunities, the additional cost is worthwhile.

Due to its popularity among house sitters Trusted Housesitters can be quite competitive. You'll need to keep on top of the email alerts for new house sits as homeowners tend to get a lot of replies in a very short amount of time.

Housecarers

- Annual Fee: $50 USD normally

- Discount: 10% off (no code needed, simply visit housesittingguide.com/sites/housecarers/)

- More Information & Reviews of Housecarers: https://www.housesittingguide.com/sites/housecarers/

Housecarers has been around for more than a decade and during that time has built up a loyal following. Based in Australia, it tends to have a lot of opportunities in the Land Down Under but also in the USA.

Housecarers is a very popular site. It's not as big as Trusted Housesitters but it's still a good place to find house sitting opportunities.

MindMyHouse

- Annual Fee: $20 USD

- More Information & Reviews of MindMyHouse: www.housesittingguide.com/sites/mind-my-house/

Although MindMyHouse isn't as proactive as Housecarers or Trusted Housesitters in implementing new features or growing the number of house sits it has, it has maintained its position as one of the top three house sitting sites. This is despite several new house sitting websites launching over the past few years.

At $20 per year, the site is extremely affordable and often a starting point for many new house sitters who want to test the waters without spending too much money.

It's not uncommon to find house sitting assignments on the site that are old or where a house sitter has already been found. The best way to avoid applying for a 'dead' house sit is to only apply for those that come in the email alerts as these are all obviously new.

Nomador

- Annual Fee: $89 USD

- More Information & Reviews of Nomador: www.housesittingguide.com/sites/nomador/

Launched in 2014, Nomador is a relatively new house sitting site. Prior to launching Nomador, the founders ran a house sitting website in France and are familiar with the market. Thanks to their previous venture, Nomador is one of the best sites to use if you're looking for house sitting opportunities in France. Nomador is also starting to do well in a number of other European countries and also in Australia where it is based.

Given that it doesn't have as many house sits as the three top sites, Nomador's membership is quite expensive. However as competition for house sits is lower than it is on other sites, it's worth considering: especially if you're looking to house sit in France or one of the other areas where it has a lot of house sits.

Nomador offer a free trial, which allows you to apply for a small handful of house sitting opportunities and get a feel for the site.

House Sit Match

- Annual Fee: From £35 (UK pounds Sterling)

- More Information & Reviews of House Sit Match: www.housesittingguide.com/sites/housesitmatch/

House Sit Match is another newcomer to the house sitting scene. The site initially focused on just the UK and Australian market but has now expanded to include house sits from all over the world, although it tends to have considerably fewer house sitting opportunities than the other sites mentioned.

House Sit Match has different pricing tiers (in pounds sterling): the most expensive costs £58.80 and the cheaper option costs £34.80.

Other House Sitting Sites

If you're planning to do the majority, or even all, of your house sitting in one country it's worth checking out some niche single-country house sitting sites. It really depends where you want to house sit, but there are a few sites covering different countries (e.g. Aussie House Sitters only covers Australia).

Generally speaking the multi-country house sitting sites like Trusted Housesitters, Housecarers and MindMyHouse tend to have the most house sitting opportunities, both worldwide and for each country. Sometimes however a smaller house sitting site will have enough opportunities to make it worth joining, especially given that you'll be competing against fewer house sitters for each house sitting assignment.

Below you will find a list of our favorite country-specific house sitting sites.

Australia-Specific House Sitting Sites

Aussie House Sitters | www.aussiehousesitters.com | $65 AUD

Mind A Home (Australia) | www.mindahome.com.au | $49 AUD

StayMe | www.stayme.com.au | $59 AUD

Happy House Sitters | www.happyhousesitters.com.au | $99 AUD

Easy House Sitting | www.easyhousesitting.com | Currently Free

Australian House Sitter | www.australianhousesitter.com.au | $30 AUD

House Sitters Australia | www.housesittersaustralia.com.au | $15 AUD

House Sit World | www.housesitworld.com.au | $50 AUD

USA-Specific House Sitting Sites

House Sitters America | www.housesittersamerica.com | $30 USD

Mind A Home (USA) | http://mindahome.com | $10 USD

UK-Specific House Sitting Sites

House Sitters UK | Housesittersuk.co.uk | £15

Mind A Home (UK) | http://mindahome.co.uk | £12

NZ-Specific House Sitting Sites

Kiwi House Sitters | www.kiwihousesitters.co.nz | $65 NZD

Mexico-Specific House Sitting Sites

House Sit Mexico | www.housesitmexico.com | $41 USD

Other places to find house sits

As mentioned previously, you'll probably find the vast majority of your house sits through house sitting sites like Trusted Housesitters or Housecarers. As you get more established, and make more contacts, you'll be able to pick up a few from word-of-mouth referrals and repeat house sits.

In the meantime, if you're proactive you can also promote yourself in the following places.

Classifieds websites

Craigslist (popular in the US), Gumtree (Popular in the UK and Australia) and Kijiji (Popular in Canada) are all places where you can advertise yourself as a house sitter, often for free. Classifieds websites tend to list the newest adverts first, so it's a good idea to post a new advert every couple of days to ensure that you're always at the top.

Expat websites

You'll notice that a lot of house sits, particularly those in Europe and South-East Asia, will be posted by English-speaking expats living in those areas. It makes sense then to advertise directly to expats as many will have pets but may not have heard about house sitting yet.

Some websites to market yourself on are:

- Angloinfo.com

- Expatforum.com

- Britishexpats.com

- Expatica.com

- Expatexchange.com

- Expatfocus.com

Repeat house sits

House sits often lead to repeat house sits. In fact, once you've house sat for a homeowner once, they'd much prefer to have you house sit for them next time, rather than advertise for a new house sitter.

Word of mouth

Word-of-mouth is a great way to land yourself more house sitting opportunities. Often when house sitting for one client, you'll end up getting introduced to other pet owners in the area.

If you're in an area that you'd like to house sit in again, get to know the neighbors. This is the easiest way to get more house sits, mainly because you won't have the same level of competition that you'd normally have on a house sitting website.

If you're in a large expat area consider getting a few business cards printed and putting them in expat bars and restaurants, local veterinary clinics and pet grooming salons. It may also be worth joining a few expat sites (e.g. Angloinfo) and posting about what you're doing, mentioning that you're new in town and would like to meet others for a coffee or a drink. Not only is it a great way to meet people but you'll be casually advertising your house sitting services as well.

It's often also worth getting in touch with a few local expat blogs or regional newspapers to tell them what you're doing. Some will find it interesting and it could lead to some useful publicity.

Set up your own website

If you start house sitting a lot, you may decide to set up your own website. Having your own website can help you to stand out from other house sitters and it may also lead to homeowners contacting you directly, rather than going through a house sitting website.

Some examples of websites include:

- Housesittingperfected.com

- http://heatherhope2.weebly.com/

You don't need to spend a lot of money to set up a house sitting website. You can even do it for free using something like WordPress, Weebly, Wix or Blogspot. The benefit of this is it's free. The only downside is that your domain name will have .WordPress or .BlogSpot in it e.g. greatlittlehousesitter.wordpress.com . If that's not an issue, then this is probably the easiest route.

If you'd like your own domain name then this will set you back around $10 a year. You'll also need to host your website which can be as cheap as a couple of dollars per month. For non-techies this can be a little confusing so perhaps the simplest way to go about this is to start with a free WordPress, Weebly or Wix website and then pay to upgrade if you decide you want your own domain name.

FAQs about house sitting sites

The following are some of the most frequently asked questions about house sitting sites.

Which site should I join?

If you're just starting out, Trusted Housesitters has the most house sitting opportunities and since you'll often have to apply for quite a few house sits before you get accepted for one (at least in the beginning), it's a good place to start.

Where you want to house sit will also impact which site you should join. Nomador for example is particularly strong in France and may be a good option if you want to do a lot of house sitting there. Australia has several Australia-specific house sitting sites such as Aussie House Sitters which may have more house sitting opportunities in Australia than some of the global house sitting sites.

It's impossible to provide a single answer that works for every reader however the following are some good questions to ask yourself about before joining a site, relevant to all readers.

- How many house sits does this site post daily, weekly and monthly?

- Is the price a fair reflection on the number of house sits?

- How many house sitters are there in comparison to house sits? (This should give you a good idea of how competitive it is likely to be.)

- Is it the best house sitting site for the region(s) I want to house sit in?

How many sites should I join?

Most people start off by joining one website and if that works out, they join a few more. After all it only takes one house sit to cover the membership cost. Most full-time house sitters are members of two to three sites.

Discount codes for house sitting sites

We have found discount codes (around 10% off) for at least two sites. We try to keep an up-to-date list here: https://www.housesittingguide.com/house-sitting-sites/

Part III: Creating Your House Sitting Profile

What are homeowners looking for?

Most house sitting websites have a place for you to create a profile. Here you'll give a little bit of information about yourself and explain why you would make a good house sitter. Although it's your application email that will create a homeowner's first impressions of you, most homeowners will also take a good look at your house sitting profile as well.

Before we get into the ins and outs of what to include in your profile, it's a good idea to try and get into the mindset of the homeowner and understand what they are and aren't looking for. The following are some of the major things homeowners look for in a house sitter. Anything you write, whether it's the content for your house sitting profile or the application email, should reflect these qualities.

Someone who loves pets

The number one reason people get a sitter is to make sure that their pets get the same love and care as they would if they were being looked after by their owners.

Homeowners aren't just looking for someone who'll take on the chores of house sitting, they want someone who really loves animals and will spend a lot of time looking after their pets and giving them the kind of attention that they're used to.

Someone who is mature, organized and reliable

Leaving your home and pets in the care of somebody else, especially a stranger, is understandably a big deal for any homeowner. Considering the homeowner will be far from the house, and it may not be possible to contact them for large periods of time, the ideal person is someone who will be organized and reliable, someone who can manage all of the house sitting responsibilities while keeping in good, regular contact with the homeowner.

Someone who is good in the event of a crisis / good at adapting

Homeowners are looking for someone who'll adapt to the surroundings of their temporary new home (and possibly country), someone who won't get homesick or be unable to cope in the event of a crisis.

Someone who's genuine

Yes, you're supposed to sell yourself but don't do so in a cheesy way. Occasionally well-meaning house sitters will describe themselves as "dream-come-true house sitters" or "the house sitters you've been waiting for".

This is the kind of language that belongs on a late night infomercial for diet pills, not for trying to convince someone who has never met you to let you stay in their home.

When homeowners read your profile, they're trying to size you up and to see if everything you write about yourself (for example that you love pets, are a keen gardener and are pretty handy at DIY) is all an exaggeration or if you are really are as good as you say you are.

Someone who can do repeat house sits if everything works out

Finding a house sitter is time-consuming for homeowners. It isn't just the process of advertising and interviewing that takes time, it's also showing the sitter how everything around the house works as well as having the pets and sitter build up a rapport together.

If the house sit goes well, most homeowners will want you to come back for any future house sits rather than go through the process of finding a new house sitter again.

What are homeowners not looking for?

Just as important as what homeowners are looking for is an overview of what homeowners are not looking for.

Someone who won't take care of the home

Even though most people have home insurance, nobody wants to come home to a house that hasn't been looked after and have to go through the hassle of dealing with the insurance company, or the hassle of trying to get the sitter to cover the cost of replacing things they've damaged.

Someone who won't take care of the pets

An even bigger concern is that the sitter won't take proper care of the pets.

Someone who is unreliable

There have been instances where house sitters have changed their minds or taken up a better offer in the weeks leading up to the start date of a house sit. The homeowner is then left to find someone at short notice, or cancel their vacation altogether.

Someone who will bail during the house sit

Thankfully this is very uncommon but there have been cases where house sitters have upped and left during a house sit.

Obviously, this is just about the worst thing a sitter can do. Finding a last minute sitter who can take over from this situation is almost impossible. More than likely the homeowner will end up having to cancel his vacation and come home. They'll also need to ask a neighbor to take care of things (such as care for the pets) while they travel home.

Someone who turns out to be a criminal

Understandably, this thought crosses the minds of a lot of homeowners.

Creating an amazing house sitter profile

(putting it all together)

The profile headline

When someone visits your profile, one of the first things that they'll notice is your profile headline. This headline should be a short and snappy sentence that sells your skills and qualities as a house sitter.

Take a look at what successful house sitters write for their profile headlines. Trusted Housesitters is a useful website for doing research as they list the sitters with the most references (i.e. those that have been getting house sits) first. Take a pen and paper, read through the profile headlines and jot down any ideas that come to mind.

You'll notice that the profiles on the first few pages all share a few common traits.

Firstly, they focus on what the sitter can offer the homeowner, rather than what the sitter wants from the homeowner. Most are a variation of "Reliable Pet Sitter With Excellent References Available To Look After Your Home & Pets", as opposed to "want to house sit in Thailand".

Secondly, these headlines make good use of words and phrases that incite trust. You'll notice a lot of the following words:

Responsible, reliable, mature, experienced, non-smoking, peace of mind, animal lover, professional, trustworthy, recommended, honest, caring...

You may also notice that a lot of these headlines say more or less the same thing but in different words. The truth is it's hard to think of something that's completely unique and that will really make you stand out from the others. If you do think of something good, chances are other people will start copying you and it won't be long before your headline is no longer unique.

Don't worry if what you come up with feels a lot like the other headlines. The important thing isn't so much that your headline stands out from the crowd but that it passes the headline check.

No homeowner has ever been won over by a headline alone. In fact, most just glance at it to see whether it's worth reading the rest of your profile (aka the headline check). Get the headline right, i.e. do what the other successful house sitters are doing, and you'll entice them to read the rest of your profile. The rest of the profile is where you can actually win them over.

Tip: If you want to make your headline stand out a little more, add something personal. Instead of just writing 'Reliable Pet Sitter With Excellent References Available To Look After Your Home & Pets' change it to 'Former Teacher With Excellent References Available To Look After Your Home & Pets'.

The profile itself

Next, you'll need to write content for the profile itself which will usually be several paragraphs summing up who you are and why homeowners should pick you as their house sitter. Some house sitting websites will have different sections, with questions for each section such as "what makes you a good house sitter". Others will leave it up to you to choose what you'll write. Regardless of how they're laid out, the following will help you to put together your house sitting profile.

Firstly, create an outline of what you want to say

Take a pen and paper, or open a word processing program like Word or Google Docs, and jot down anything you can say about the following topics.

Pets

- Have you pet sat before (even if it's just for friends or family)?

- Have you owned pets before?

- Do you love pets?

Who you are

Although the best advice for creating a house sitting profile is to focus on what you can offer the homeowner, rather than what you want from the homeowner, it's a good idea to share a little bit of your personality and who you are as well. Your hobbies, passions, and why you've started house sitting are all good things to mention. Adding a few personal lines can really help you to make a connection with the homeowner and help your profile stand out from the others.

Home & garden care experience

Note: Be honest. Although it's tempting to exaggerate your handyman skills or how much you love animals, it's always better to be honest instead.

- Are you tidy?

- Are you handy around the house?

- Have you owned a property before?

- Will you treat someone else's home like your own?

- Have you gardening experience?

- Have you ever owned - and cleaned - a pool before?

Signs of maturity

Homeowners are looking for reliable, mature sitters. If you're under thirty, you will probably find that your age will make some homeowners think twice before allowing you to house sit for them. This isn't to say that it's impossible to get a house sit if you're under thirty, some of the most successful sitters are in their twenties, however it's a hurdle that you'll have to overcome.

If you're a non-smoker or a non-drinker, it's a good idea to mention this as well.

Why do you want to house sit?

Most house sitting sites will ask you why you want to house sit. Let's be honest here, it's for the free accommodation. Although there are other benefits to house sitting, this is the main reason that people start house sitting. What's amazing is that very few people admit this in their profiles and try to come up with some altruistic reason instead.

At the end of the day, homeowners know that you're not doing this solely out of the goodness of your heart. Admitting that you're house sitting because you want to see the world and want to be able to do that on a budget is perfectly acceptable. If anything, it'll help you to come across as more genuine.

Travel experience

Language skills, familiarity with certain cultures and experience travelling or living abroad are all worth mentioning. If you're applying for a house sit in France for example, the homeowner is likely to be most interested in applicants that have some knowledge of French.

Are you responsible?

- Have you held a job with a reasonable amount of responsibility?

- Have you run your own business before?

Traditional jobs such as lawyers, bank managers and teachers tend to go down particularly well as the responsibility they entail is obvious. If your job isn't one of these, you should give a few details about the responsibility involved in this job.

Next, write it

Very simply, get it down. Don't worry if it's nowhere near perfect the first time round. The most important thing is to get it written. Writing is rewriting as they say. You can always go back and edit it later.

Remember, a good introductory paragraph is key

Homeowners will often review many profiles when they're deciding on who their house sitter should be and often won't make it past the first paragraph. It's a good idea to sum up all of the good points about you in this paragraph so that you can entice them to read more.

The profile photo(s)

They say you should never judge a book by its cover but in reality most people do. Homeowners are definitely guilty of this as most profiles that don't have photos, or don't have very good ones, tend not to get picked for house sits.

The following are some of the top tips to get the most mileage from your photos:

Upload as many photos as the site allows

- Most house sitting sites allow you to include several photos in your profile. Make sure you upload as many as the site allows.

Include at least one close up

- Make sure at least one of the photos is a close-up.

- Don't wear sunglasses, a hat or anything that hides your face too much.

- Also don't forget to smile!

Include at least one group shot (if needed)

- If you're a couple or family make sure there's at least one photo of you all together.

- Have at least one photo that includes a pet

- At least one of your photos should include a pet as part of the picture.

- If you don't have a photo of you with a pet, it's worthwhile borrowing one just for the photo.

- Along with photos of pets, it's also a good idea to have photos of you doing typical house sitting tasks such as gardening or cleaning the pool.

Don't upload any photos that make you look unprofessional

•   Homeowners don't want a party animal staying in their property. Even a photo of you with a glass of wine can be enough to turn some homeowners off.

Pay special attention to your main photo

- Most sites allow you to select one photo as your main photo.

- This photo will usually be the photo that appears in the search result pages when homeowners search for a sitter and it will also be the first photo a homeowner sees when they go on your profile.

- This photo should be a friendly photo, where everyone is smiling.

- If you're house sitting as a couple or family, make sure you're all in it.

- There should be a pet or two in the photo as well.

The profile video

If a picture is a thousand words, a video is easily a hundred thousand. Unlike a photo, a video isn't required on most house sitting websites. But even though it's not required, and even though plenty of house sitters get house sits without one, a video can make a connection with a homeowner in a way that a photo never can.

Yvonne & Michael Bauche recently spoke to housesittingguide.com about a house sit they took on in St Lucia. When applying for that particular house sit, they sent the homeowners a link to their video and after watching it, the owners replied offering the house sit to them. Just watching the video meant the owners felt like the owners already knew Yvonne & Michael and were happy to consider them as house sitters straight away. (There were 80 other applicants within the first four hours of posting).

It's easy to make a video. All you need to shoot the video is a camera phone or a webcam and the video itself only needs to be 2-3 minutes of you talking about yourself.

The following are some tips for shooting a house sitter video:

- It doesn't have to be long

- In fact, try to keep it to less than three minutes.

- You don't need fancy equipment

- A smartphone or webcam is fine. Don't worry if the picture quality isn't perfect. What matters most is that homeowners get a good sense of who you are.

Have some idea of what you're going to say

You don't need to write a script but having a couple of pointers to refer to can make things easier. If you're not sure what to say, simply re-word what you wrote in your house sitter profile. Try to put those prompts behind the camera so you're not looking down at the floor or coffee table every few seconds.

Be careful recording outside

Poor sound quality is worse than having poor video quality. Recording inside is generally better as recording outside can make it harder for people to hear what you're saying.

If you record inside make sure there's reasonable lighting

Make sure that you're clearly visible and that viewers won't have to strain their eyes to see you. You may want to make a test video to check that the quality of the picture is good.

If you're a couple or family make sure everyone is in the video

As with photos, everyone who's going to be house sitting should be in the video. Homeowners will want to get a sense of everyone (kids and pets included) who might be staying in their home.

Don't be too nervous

It's easier said than done of course but try to ignore the camera and focus on being as natural and friendly as possible.

Getting references

Having references makes a big difference when applying for house sits. Even if everything else on your profile is perfect, most homeowners will be extremely hesitant to take you on if you don't have any references. The more references you have, the easier you'll find it is to get accepted for house sitting assignments.

Getting a house sit without any references is difficult. Obviously you won't be able to get any house sitting references until you house sit, but there are a few ways to get other references - references that are good enough for most homeowners - without house sitting first.

Previous landlords

Have you rented a property recently? A reference from a previous landlord shows that you are responsible and can be trusted to look after a home. This is obviously relevant to house sitting.

Previous employers

Are you able to get a reference from a current or previous job?

There's no need to include a reference for every single job you've ever had, just focus on the jobs where you held some degree of responsibility.

Character references

Do you know someone who can give you a character reference? Technically just about anyone can give you a character reference but it'll mean a lot more if it comes from someone in a traditional career such as a teacher, lawyer, bank manager or doctor.

Other reference-based websites

Profiles on any of the following websites can help to show that you're a real, trustworthy person:

- LinkedIn - especially if you have references on your profile.

- Apartment rental websites such as Airbnb, Housetrip or Wimdu - again, especially useful if you have references.

- Hospitality exchange websites such as Couchsurfing or BeWelcome.

- Home swapping websites such as Homeexchange.com or Lovehomeswap.

How to get even more references

References from employers and landlords are good but obviously a reference for actually having house sat is worth a lot more. The following are some of the quickest and easiest ways to get more relevant references.

Offer to house sit for friends & family

Get in touch with all of your friends and family members that have pets and let them know that you're available to house sit, even if it's just for a single night. You'll be surprised at how many people will take you up on the offer.

Of course if you've ever looked after a friend or neighbor's pets before, get in touch and ask them to write a reference for you.

Apply for local house sits

Keep an eye on house sits in your area. Homeowners are far more likely to let a newbie house sitter look after their home and pets if they can meet them first.

Even though your dream house sits might not be in your own back yard, house sitting in your own town or city can be just as enjoyable as house sitting abroad, especially if it's a neighborhood you've never lived in before.

Apply for house sit in places you've already visited

Ryan Biddulph had already been to Bali four times before he applied for a house sit in Bali and this, he believes, was a big factor in him getting the house sit. (Ryan's Interview: http://www.housesittingguide.com/?p=1188)

Although you may be tempted to apply for house sits in locations you've never visited before, there's a big benefit to applying for house sits in places you already know. Homeowners are usually more willing to take on somebody if they are already familiar with that country.

Apply for urgent / last-minute house sits

Homeowners have to be less-picky when it comes to last-minute house sits. There are also generally fewer other people applying, as most people won't be able to drop everything and travel quickly. If you're in the position of being able to, this is a very easy way to get accepted for a house sit and get a good reference to your name.

WWOOF

WWOOFing, otherwise known as working on organic farms, is a concept that's been around since the 1970s.In return for working on a farm (usually for around 4 hours a day), the owners give you your board and usually at least one cooked meal per day.

If you're already on the road, WWOOFing can be a great way to get some references, and those references will be particularly useful if you take on jobs that involve looking after animals. It's also a fun way to travel and definitely worth trying at least once.

Pet sit in your own home

There are a number of new websites where you can sign up to look after other people's pets in your home, and get paid for it. This a great opportunity to both earn some extra cash and also a good way to get some relevant references and experience as well.

Some of the main sites to look at are DogVacay, Rover and Pawshake.com.

Get a sitter

Go away for a break and have a sitter come look after your home or pets. If you're able to say that you've been a homeowner that's taken on house sitters before, you will make a really good connection with other homeowners as you'll understand what it's like to be in their shoes.

Volunteer at an animal charity

Animal charities are always looking for extra pairs of hands. Having that kind of reference on your profile shows that you really are an animal lover.

Background checks

Many house sitting sites will ask you whether or not you have a background check. In most countries this background check simply checks that you have no criminal records and provides you with a letter stating this. It's fairly easy to get a hold of - usually it's just a case of going into your local police station and requesting it. There's usually a small admin fee involved.

Although most homeowners never ask to see this, the fact that you have one will help to put their mind at ease. You'll find that having one makes a big difference in how likely you are to get accepted for a house sit.

Below are some links with more information about the procedures for getting a background check in various countries:

- USA:
  http://travel.state.gov/content/passports/english/abroad/legal-matters/criminal-record-check.html

- UK (excluding Scotland): https://www.gov.uk/copy-of-police-records

- Scotland:
  http://www.disclosurescotland.co.uk/basicdisclosureonline/index.htm

- Canada:

  http://www.rcmp-grc.gc.ca/cr-cj/fing-empr2-eng.htm

- Australia:

  http://www.afp.gov.au/what-we-do/police-checks/national-police-checks.aspx

- New Zealand:

  http://www.justice.govt.nz/services/criminal-records

- Ireland:
  http://www.garda.ie/Controller.aspx?Page=2742&Lang=1

- South Africa:
  http://www.saps.gov.za/services/applying_clearence_certific
  ate.php

Bonus suggestion:

Get a pet first aid certificate

One thing very few house sitters have is a pet first aid certificate. It's certainly not a requirement but naturally having one could help your profile to really stand out.

A pet first aid course will teach you skills such as:

- Pet CPR

- Treating wounds

- Caring for specific injuries (such as eye, foot and ear injuries)

- Administering medicine to pets

- Dealing with emergency situations

Most pet first aid courses take place over a day or a weekend, however there are also an increasing number of online courses. Below are just a few of the different organizations that provide pet first aid training.

USA

http://www.walksnwags.com/firstaiddates.php (Northern USA)

http://www.pettech.net/petsaver.php

Canada

http://www.sja.ca/English/Courses-and-Training/Pages/Course%20Descriptions/Pet-First-Aid.aspx

http://www.walksnwags.com/firstaiddates.php

http://www.dogsafe.ca/courses2.html

UK

http://www.animalaiders.co.uk

http://www.reflexfirstaidtraining.co.uk/courses/canine-first-aid/

http://www.dog-first-aid.com

Australia

http://www.pettech.net.au/

New Zealand

http://www.petfirstaidandtrainingnz.co.nz/pet-first-aid-and-traning-courses-dates

Online

https://www.udemy.com/first-aid-for-pets/

http://www.britishcollegeofcaninestudies.com/product/canine-first-aid-course/

http://www.dogsafe.ca/courses2.html (distance learning)

Applying For House Sits

A couple of questions to ask yourself

So you've found a house sit you like. That's fantastic! Before you apply for it, here a couple of questions you should ask yourself.

While there's no harm in just getting an email sent and then thinking about it properly later, it is good to think about the following before progressing too far down the application stage. These are all questions the homeowner is likely to ask you as well.
Questions to ask yourself

- Will you need a VISA to enter this country?

- Can you stay in that country for the length of the house sit?

- If you work will you need to get time off work?

- Can you definitely do this?

Questions about the house sit

- How much will it cost to get there? (Note: See the chapter on finding cheap flights)

- How many hours per day do you estimate the responsibilities will take?

- Are these responsibilities you're comfortable handling?

- How's the WIFI? (This is a big consideration if you're a freelancer).

- Do you actually like the location?

- Are there things to see and do nearby?

- How much would this cost me to rent through somewhere

like Airbnb? (If it's cheap are you better off renting?)

- Will you need a vehicle while you're there or to get there? (Sometimes a car will be provided while other times you'll need to rent one. Be sure to check your driving license will be valid).

- Are you being asked to cover the utility costs, and if so is it still a good deal? (Most homeowners won't ask you to cover these costs but a few will).

- Are you okay with the weather conditions that there are likely to be during the house sit? (E.g. is it during the cold season, the hot season or the rainy season?)

- What will your cost of living be while you're there? (You can get an idea of grocery and restaurant prices at Numbeo.com)

- Why are the owners going away? (Often, particularly for longer term house sits, there's a good reason the owners are going away such as poor weather).

- How big is the house? (Big houses mean more cleaning).

Questions about the pets

- What care do they need?

- Are there any restrictions on how long they can be left alone in the house?

- Do the pets require medication? If so, how frequently per day?

- How old are the pets?

Top Tip: If you don't get accepted for the house sit, be polite and let the homeowner know that you're still available if the other sitter changes their mind. Never burn your bridges. Charli Moore applied for a house sit in St Kitts but even though she was ideal for the job, the homeowners felt they would rather go with a more mature couple. In the end, the other couple fell through and Charli was offered the house sit instead. (Charli's Interview: http://www.housesittingguide.com/?p=1201)

This isn't uncommon. Rob & Nat took on their house sit in Thailand when the other house sitters fell through. (Rob & Nat's Interview: http://www.housesittingguide.com/?p=1193)

Applying for the house sit

Be quick

It's good to apply for house sits as quickly as possible. Often homeowners will get inundated with emails, particularly when the daily emails for that day go out. These emails get sent out to several hundred or even thousand people at once and so around this time homeowners will often get a big bunch of applications all in one go.

You ideally want to get your application email seen before they get to that stage.

Have a tweakable template

Applying for house sits takes time and although your application email will be slightly different for every house sit, you'll notice each application email will have a lot of similarities.

It's good to have a rough template that you can tweak for each assignment and keep saved on your computer or in a Google Doc. This will save you a lot of time and will ensure that you always send a good application e-mail.

Don't worry if you repeat a lot of what's in your house sitting profile. Some homeowners won't click through to the profiles and so will base your applications solely on the emails that you send. Just make sure the email isn't too long and is broken up into easy-to-read paragraphs.

In terms of tweaking, the first paragraph should always be specific to that house sit as it'll show you've read through the requirements of that house sit.

Tell homeowners a little bit about yourself

A lot of application emails say all of the right things e.g. the sitters are animal lovers, they're responsible, they're non-smokers etc. These are all great things to write in your application email but if that's all you write, there won't be anything to distinguish you from the tens of other applications the homeowner receives.

Along with saying all of the right things, make sure you tell the homeowner a little bit about who you are. Are you retired? What do you do for a living? Why are you house sitting? What specifically attracts you to that particular house sit?

The key here is to make a connection and the first step to making a connection is to tell homeowners a little bit about who you are.

Don't forget the pets

Be sure to mention the pets (by name if the names are mentioned in the house sitting adverts). Pets are after all the number one reason people get a house sitter.

For example if the house sit includes the responsibility of looking after a Labrador named Charlie and you have experience of either owning a dog or looking after one, mention that in the email. If you've looked after Labradors before, mention that as well.

You can also get a good mention of the pets in the subject line e.g. "Trustworthy Pet Sitters Available to Look after Charlie".

Heidi and Alan Wagoner gave up their lives in America and decides to travel the world with their kids. Recently they took on a house sit in Kuala Lumpur, Malaysia. Speaking to housesittingguide.com about their house sit, they believe it was a comment they made about the pets in their initial application email that made them stand out as house sitters.

"They said it was our comment in our original application that drew them to us. They had posted a photo of Luke (dog) and Lucky (cat) and we made mention of them matching and looking good together. It was a genuine comment about their pets and that made it personal."

Mention qualifications specific to that house sit

If you're well-suited to that particular house sit for example if you speak the language of that country or if you've looked after that type of pet before, mention that as soon as possible. This will help to ensure you get shortlisted for the next stage of interviews.

Be brief but concise

Don't write an essay but don't be so brief that you don't mention anything of value. Writing a short but concise email is easier said than done which is why it helps to have a template that you can tweak when applying for house sits.

Give other contact details

Often the messaging systems on house sitting websites aren't very good and it's much easier to take the conversation over to email, or even better to a phone call or Skype. Phone calls are much better for making a personal connection than emails so if there's ever an option between the two, always choose the phone call. If you're in a different time zone to the homeowner, suggest a time that would be convenient to you both (but especially convenient to them).

Try to get their name

It isn't always possible but if you can get a name for the homeowner this always helps to make a difference. In fact making any kind of personal connection goes a long way.

Simon and Donna noticed that the homeowners had lived in Europe previously and as that was a common connection, they mentioned it in their application email. Even though this was just a small offhand comment, it helped them make a connection with the homeowners and ultimately to get accepted for the house sit. (Simon & Donna's Interview: http://www.housesittingguide.com/?p=668)

Consider offering to meet the homeowner first

Depending on the value of the house sit to you, if you're really interested in doing the house sit, offering to meet the homeowner first will make a big difference as to how likely you are to get the house sit.

Obviously this isn't practical for all house sits, but if the travel costs are reasonable (comparative to the value of the house sit) and the distance isn't too far, it's a worthwhile consideration if you are looking for an easy way to increase your chances of getting that house sit.

Follow up after a day or two

Be aware that homeowners will receive a lot of emails in the days that follow posting a house sitting assignment and it may take a couple of days for them to reply. If you haven't heard anything back after a couple of days, feel free to follow up.

Don't take rejection personally

It's all part of the process. The more house sitting you do, the less you'll end up getting rejected. Also, as mentioned previously in this book, often there isn't a good reason why you were rejected. Homeowners will often have a shortlist of many excellent sitters to choose from and will either pick one randomly or go with their gut.

Phone calls & Skype

After a couple of emails back and forth, if the homeowner is strongly considering you they'll usually arrange a phone call or Skype call.

These days the majority of interviews take place over Skype. It's cheaper for international calls and also it gives the homeowners a chance to see you and often to give you a virtual tour of their home. So if you don't have a webcam, consider getting one.

As with normal job interviews, it's always good to have some questions to ask as this shows you're prepared. In any case you should always ask a couple of questions about the pets.

If you don't already know exactly where the property is, most homeowners are okay with giving out their address or a rough address at this point. This will then help you to work out whether the house sit is in a location you'd like to visit.

Although the phone call is normally for the homeowner to get a good idea of who you are, it's also there for you to get a better impression of the homeowner. Ask yourself whether they'll be easy to get along with or to work with if there are any issues.

If you're happy and this is a house sit you'd definitely like to do, it's a good idea to say that you're happy to book your transportation to the house sit (e.g. flights) and forward them the details once done as this helps to show how reliable you are.

If possible (and this will depend on your car situation during the house sit), let the homeowners know that you're happy to give them a lift to the airport if needed.

The house sitting agreement

A house sitting agreement is usually little more than the details of the house sit (e.g. start date, end date etc.), a list of responsibilities during the house sit and a few contacts in case there's an emergency.

For house sitters the value of a house sitting agreement isn't so much as a legal document. Rather it's helpful to sitters because it encourages homeowners to think of all the responsibilities involved and to get them down on paper.

The more detailed the responsibilities are the better e.g. walk the dogs daily for 45 minutes is better than just walk the dog as it helps the house sitter to size up how much work is involved on a daily or weekly basis.

It's a good idea to get your house sitting agreement, and any other documents such as checklists, filled in before the handover starts. By the time you arrive for the handover, the homeowner(s) will be in another world. Their minds will be a little all over the place and so they're more likely to forget to tell you a few things. As soon as the house sit is agreed upon, start collecting all of this information from the homeowner. Keep reminding them as the date draws nearer and make sure that you have all of the information you need by at least the week before the house sit starts.

Some things you should definitely get agreed upon (either through the house sitting agreement or otherwise):

- The responsibilities: In order to know exactly how much work is involved, it's much better to have this written down and agreed upon.

- The dates of the house sit: When the homeowners will leave and return.

- The dates of the handover: When you'll arrive for the handover and how long this will be for. There's usually a handover at the end as well, although this is often as short as an hour or two.

- The homeowner's rough itinerary: This is useful in case you need to contact them during the house sit.

- Who will pay what: Ideally you'll want an emergency float that you can dip into in the case of an emergency. It's also good to have an agreement that if you incur any costs, the homeowner will reimburse you.

- What costs, if any, the house sitter has to pay: Some homeowners ask you to pay towards things like utilities.

- Security deposit: It's not common for homeowners to ask for a security deposit but occasionally homeowners do. Never pay this before arriving at a house sit. Instead offer to transfer it during the handover period.

Quick Check

Have you:

- Booked your flights (or other transport) to the house sit? You should let the homeowner know once you have done this.

- Do you have the address of the property? Often rural house sits are difficult to find and aren't always on Google Maps or Sat Nav. You should always ask the homeowner for directions rather than solely rely on technology.

- Do you have a copy of the homeowner's contact details in case you get lost?

- Do you know what time the homeowner is expecting you on the day of the handover? Have you given yourself some leeway?

- Have you arranged travel insurance? Some people travel with it, others don't. It's entirely up to you.

During The House Sit

The pre-house sit handover

Every house sit has two handovers, one before the house sit begins and one after it ends. How long the handovers last depends on the length of the house sit. For medium or long term house sits, the pre-house sit handover usually lasts a day or two. For shorter-term house sits, it may only last a couple of hours although often homeowners will invite you for dinner and so it'll include an overnight as the homeowner's guest.

Set dates for the handover in advance

It's a good idea to agree on the dates of the handover in advance, ideally when you get offered the house sit and agree to take it.

Try to avoid committing to handovers that are longer than a day or two in length. Even for long term house sits, this is more than enough time for the homeowners to show you everything that you need to know. Any longer than this and you'll probably find yourself getting under the homeowner's feet.

If a homeowner asks for longer, politely suggest otherwise. If it's their first time having house sitters they're probably doing so because they don't know how much time they will need.

Bring a gift

If a homeowner invites you to dinner, it's a nice idea to bring a gift. It doesn't need to be anything extravagant. Flowers, chocolates or a bottle of wine all work perfectly.

Take lots of notes

Depending on the house sit, you may be fed a lot of information in a very short amount of time. It's a good idea to take as many notes as possible and for more complicated instructions, use a digital camera or camera phone to make a short video.

Not only does this mean you're less likely to need to contact the homeowner while they're travelling, but it will also make you look more thorough and organized.

Get to know the neighbors

During the handover try to meet at least one of the neighbors and the point of contact, if that isn't also a neighbor. If something goes wrong during the house sit, this is the person you'll need to speak to.

It's important to highlight that the point of contact isn't someone who's just there for emergencies. They're there to answer all of your questions, rather than you getting in touch with the homeowner. In fact homeowners will feel more relaxed if they know you're in good communication with the point of contact and that you'll get in touch with them if you need anything.

Neighbors, particularly in smaller communities, like to know what's going on and it's always a good idea to introduce yourself to them.

Get to know the pets

It's a good idea that you feed the pets and walk them while you're there, even if you're doing these chores alongside the homeowner. This will give the pets a chance to get you know you and you to get to know the pets.

Get to know your routine

If you're there for a full day, practice doing your routine while the homeowner is there. Again, this is a good chance to show how diligent you are but even more importantly it's a good opportunity to see how accurate the homeowner's instructions actually are while the homeowner is still there.

Get to know the area

While you're there on the handover ask the homeowner to show you where the following places are:

- The hospital

- The veterinary clinic

- The supermarket

- Where to get a taxi (and useful phone numbers for this)

- The gas station

- The police station

Don't forget

Have you asked about...

- Turning off the water

- Turning off the electricity

- The internet (make sure you get a password for this)

- When the garbage gets collected

- When the plants should be watered

While house sitting

Keep up regular contact

Some homeowners like regular contact while others prefer not to be disturbed on their vacation. During the handover, you should be able to get a feel for what type of person they are but if in doubt, just ask what they'd prefer. Regardless of which type of person they are, it's a good idea to send a few emails during the first few days, just to let them know that you're settling in without any problems.

In terms of problems or questions, it's always better to ask the homeowner rather than try and sort things blindly. The temptation may be to try not to disturb the homeowner at all, particularly with small problems, but most will be really happy you asked.

At this point you should also be in touch with the point of contact, and asking them questions. Homeowners will feel more at ease, and will be more likely to trust you to do your thing, if they know that you're in touch with the point of contact.

When contacting the homeowner, do so by e-mail. If you phone, homeowners are likely to think it's an emergency and you'll worry them unnecessarily.

Often, there won't be anything to report on. In these cases, sending through a photo of the pets, particularly if they've done something cute, is a good way to maintain that contact.

Get into a routine

Try to get into a routine for each house sit e.g. walk the dogs first, then feed the cats etc. It's not essential but it does help to ensure all of the chores get done each day. It's also worth putting a list of chores somewhere obvious such as on the refrigerator, and making sure they get done each day.

Lock the doors and windows

Some homeowners can be very relaxed about potential crime and will tell you not to bother locking the doors or windows, however it's always better to err on the side of caution and lock them each time you leave the house.

Don't move things around too much

Most homeowners like to come back to find things exactly how they left them, even if your new arrangement is better.

If you do decide to move furniture, make sure you take a photo of how everything was laid out first, so that you can put it all back together at the end of the house sit.

Be honest about damages

During a house sit things sometimes break, especially wine glasses. Do try to replace these if you know where the homeowner bought them, or offer to pay for them if you don't.

Never try to hide any breakages or damages.

Don't be nosy

Although many homeowners will do their best to tidy up anything that's confidential, there will often be a lot of items that are personal to the homeowner lying around the house. Treat the home as you would hope other house sitters would behave in your home and don't pry.

Organize the mail

Keep all the mail so the homeowners can look through it when they return.

A nice idea is to try to organize it in order so the owners can look at the oldest (and by that point most urgent) letters first and by stacking anything that looks like junk mail into another pile.

If anyone phones, email a message to the homeowners

If there are any phone calls or house visits, take a message and send the message and phone number to the homeowner by email.

Keep a note of everything for the end of house sit report

It's certainly not a requirement, but putting everything important into an end of house sit report, can be very helpful to homeowners and again, shows how organized you are.

The report doesn't need to be anything fancy. Just create a Word document on your computer at the start of the house sit and any time anything worth noting happens, for example if someone phones and leaves a message or if anything unusual happens with the pets, make a note of it along with a date of when it happened. Even though you'll often be e-mailing the homeowners about this at the time, this document is a nice touch and shows your professionalism and thoroughness.

Preparing for the homeowner's return

As the house sit comes to an end, you should begin to prepare for the homeowner's return.

Do a big clean

You'll want to make sure that the house is spotless for the homeowner's return. The big clean is a big part of every house sitting assignment and takes anything from a couple of hours to a whole day, depending on how fast you are and how big the house is. If you can afford it, you might want to hire a professional cleaner to do the work for you. If you're looking after a particularly luxurious property, chances are the owner (or their neighbors) will already know a few suitable people.

Offer to pick them up from the airport

Offering to pick the homeowners up from the airport (assuming it's practical) is a nice gesture and one they'll certainly appreciate. You can also let them know that you're willing to do this before the house sit starts.

Prepare a meal for the homeowners

A lot of house sitters cook dinner for the homeowners upon their return, which we think is a lovely gesture.

You'll get a feel for whether this is a good idea or not. Some homeowners will really appreciate the effort while others might be masterchefs who would rather cook for themselves or order in. Another option is to bake (or buy) a cake which you can serve with tea and coffee when the homeowner returns. Flowers and a thank you note also go a long way.

Stock up the fridge

It's nice to leave a couple of essentials such as milk, eggs and bread for the homeowner's return. Feel free to ask them if there's anything additional they'd like.

Finally

Strip the bed and, if you have time, wash the sheets as well. Don't forget to leave the keys somewhere obvious so that you don't leave with them.

The post house sit handover

Once the homeowners return, they'll usually want to spend at least a couple of hours with you, hearing how everything went. Depending on how long the house sit you've just finished was, the handover can last anything from around twenty minutes (best suited to a short house sit) or overnight (at the end of a six month sit).

Here you can show them your house sit report (if you've made one) and let them know if there were any problems. It's also a good opportunity to mention how much a reference would mean to you and to ask if it's okay if you request one in the next few days. Most homeowners will naturally say yes.

Generally speaking, after returning from their trip most homeowners will want to relax or settle back into their life. Don't rush out the door but also don't prolong the handover any longer than is needed.

Staying in Touch

The house sit might be over, and you may even have already received a reference, but that doesn't mean it's time to break off contact with the homeowner. Most homeowners once they find a house sitter they like will want that house sitter to come back and house sit for them again and again. If you enjoyed the house sit, and would like to do another house sit there, then it's a good idea to keep in contact with the homeowner.

Christmas is the obvious time to send an out-of-the-blue email or card. Some house sitters also send a thank you card a couple of days or weeks after the house sit.

Another nice idea is to send an email with a cute photo of the pets, 3 or 6 months after the house sit is over. Most house sitters constantly snap photos of the pets, so finding one shouldn't be hard.

Along with the homeowner, it's also often sending at least a Christmas email to the point of contact for that house sit. Since they already know that you're a reliable house sitter, it makes sense to stay in touch with them just in case they ever need a house sitter (or know anyone else who does).

Other House Sitting Info

Long term house sitting

For anyone who wants to travel full-time, a long-term house sit is the holy grail of house sitting. It's possible to find house sitting assignments that last from two months to as much as two years, particularly during the off-season periods.

Long-term house sits are great for a number of reasons:

- Free accommodation on a long-term basis.

- The travel costs of doing one long term house sit are cheaper than several short term house sits.

- Staying in one place for a long period of time gives you a chance to really get a feel for it and live like a local rather than a tourist.

- If you're staying in a non-English-speaking country, you'll have a good opportunity to learn the language.

- Of course there are a few cons to long term house sits as well:

- You're limited to one location.

- Saying goodbye to the pets is even harder at the end.

Where to find long term house sits

Long term house sits crop up on every single house sitting website. One option is to just keep an eye on them all. Most send out a daily or weekly e-mail with their latest house sits and so if you subscribe to them all, you'll find out whenever there are any new long term house sitting assignments available.

Of course this is quite time consuming. Alternatively, The following guide shows you how to filter the house sits on each of the different house sitting websites so that they only show the long term house sits: http://www.housesittingguide.com/faqs/long-term-house-sits/

Applying for a long term house sit

Applying for a long term house sit is just like applying for a short-term house sit, although more emphasis should be placed on your ability to adapt to living in a new location for a long period of time.

In your application email, it's a good idea to mention any other previous long term house sits you've done (if any). If you've lived abroad, or moved to a new area before, it's also worth mentioning that.

Also worth including is a brief paragraph as to why you want to live in that particular area for so long. Do you want to learn the language? Have you always been interested in the culture? A long term house sit will have a lot of applications from prospective sitters, but if you can show that you really want to live in that particular area (and aren't just applying because you want free accommodation for six months) you stand a much better chance of getting it.

Going away for a night or two during a long term house sit

It depends on the length of the house sit but with particularly lengthy ones it may be possible to arrange with the homeowners so that you can go away for a night or two. Usually the owner will have friends or family that will be willing to pet sit for a night or two; they just weren't able to commit to the full length of the long term house sit. This should all be arranged in advance so that the homeowner can make arrangements with the neighbor or friend before the house sit begins.

It's a good idea to mention this during the application stage as it shows that you've thought about the ins and outs of a long term house sit.

House sitting as a family

House sitting works well for families. Firstly, you get a lot more space than most families who travel are used to. Secondly, you'll save a lot of money on accommodation and dining costs. Finally, having pets around can help to keep the children entertained.

Unfortunately you will find that quite a few homeowners will choose single people and couples over families.

Trusted Housesitters is a good site for families to use as it allows homeowners to select whether they would accept a family as their house sitters or not. When looking at the latest house sits, you can use the advanced search feature to only include those that accept sitters travelling with children.

For other websites, you may need to apply for each house sit individually. Once they respond to you you'll find out if they're family-friendly.

House sitting for digital nomads

A digital nomad is someone who can work their job from anywhere in the world as long as there is a good internet connection.

House sitting works well for digital nomads and digital nomads make great house sitters. Because digital nomads and freelancers have to work during the day, they'll be spending a lot more time in the house. This keeps the pets company and also helps to ward off burglars.

House sitting works great for digital nomads. Aside from all of the usual benefits such as free accommodation, having a great place to stay and having pets to look after, the following are some other benefits that apply to remote workers.

Benefits of house sitting for digital nomads

There's often enough room for an office

Working and living in the same room gets tiring after a while and it's nice to be able to separate the two. House sitting often means looking after a home with more bedrooms than you need and so you'll have the opportunity to turn one into an office.

Having a desk

Most homes have a desk to work from which is considerably easier than being hunched over a table in a coffee shop all day.

Stay in big, expensive cities

Sydney, London, New York and San Francisco are all great areas to be a digital nomad in but also some of the most expensive cities in the world. Thankfully, there are an increasing number of house sits in those areas and house sitting makes it possible to stay there without incurring huge accommodation costs.

Challenges of house sitting for digital nomads

Internet connections

Finding a good internet connection is a challenge anywhere. Most digital nomads spend half their life with their fingers crossed, hoping the internet connection at the next place is going to be okay.

With house sitting you have the benefit of being able to ask homeowners about the internet connection, something you can't usually do when booking a hotel or a hostel. Unfortunately not everybody knows what 'good' means and you'll often have to clarify.

It's a good idea to double check the internet connection isn't a dongle, as this is common in remote areas. If the homeowner is unsure as to whether the connection is good enough for your needs, ask them to test the speed of the connection using speedtest.net.

Handover days

Most house sits require a day or two of handover at the beginning of the house sit and a couple of hours to a day at the other end.

Unfortunately, this often ends up falling on a work day. If you have clients, you will need to schedule your calls to another day. If you don't have clients but still have work to do, you'll have to make it up on another day.

Making friends during house sits

Travel can be lonely and house sitting is no exception, particularly if you're house sitting on a long term basis. The following websites can be useful for making friends whilst house sitting.

Couchsurfing.org

Couchsurfing.org generally attracts a younger crowd (20s-30s), although you will find people of all ages using it. Most major cities have regular couchsurfing events and meetups where you can meet other people. It's also possible to search for people who are nearby and message them directly to see if they'd like to meet for a coffee or a beer.

Site: https://www.couchsurfing.com

Meetup

Meetup.com is a website aimed at making it easy to meet new people. The groups are usually centered around an activity for example walking, learning languages or playing sports.

Meetup tends to be most popular in cities so you may not find many groups if you're house sitting in a rural location.

Site: http://www.meetup.com

Expat websites

Expat websites such as Angloinfo can also be a good place to meet up with other people. A simple forum post introducing yourself, letting people know why you're in the area and inviting others to meet for a coffee or a beer is often all it takes to get connected to some people in the area.

Language exchanges

Language exchanges can be a good way to meet other people. There are several language exchange websites which connect language learners with native speakers, particularly where there's a mutual benefit. So for example, if you're a native English speaker who's learning Spanish you'll be able to see native Spanish speakers who are learning English and connect with them.

If you're living somewhere where English isn't the main language, a language exchange is a great opportunity to meet new people, get better insights into the culture and hopefully get a better grasp of the language as well.

Some useful websites include:

- Conversationexchange.com

- Mylanguageexchange.com

- Interpals.net

FAQs about house sitting

The following are some of the most common questions asked about house sitting that aren't already answered elsewhere in this book.

Can friends come to visit?

This depends on what you've agreed with the homeowner beforehand. Whether or not the homeowner will agree varies from house sit to house sit. It's more commonly allowed with long term house sits than with short term house sits.

How far in advance do house sits get posted?

The majority of house sits are posted a couple of months before they are due to take place but there are also usually plenty of last minute house sitting opportunities at any given time as well.

Long term house sits tend to be posted quite far in advance as taking a trip of more than two months usually takes a lot of planning on the homeowner's part and isn't something that's usually done spontaneously.

How much should I budget for travel costs?

Again this varies from house sit to house sit. At the very least you'll need to factor in the costs of getting to the house sit (see our chapter on finding cheap flights) and your living costs during the house sit, which can be as little as just your grocery shopping costs.

If you need to estimate the cost of groceries or meals out, Numbeo.com is a useful resource.

Can I house sit with a pet?

This varies from homeowner to homeowner. If the homeowner is potentially okay with having you house sit with your pet, they'll usually want to meet you and the pet first so that they can see how your pet interacts with theirs.

What if I need to cancel?

If you need to cancel, the most helpful thing that you can do is contact the homeowners immediately. Finding a new house sitter takes time and you should give the homeowner as much time as possible to do it.

It goes without saying that you should only cancel if you have a genuinely good reason and not that you've found another, better house sit.

What if the homeowner cancels on me?

Homeowners cancelling on sitters is rare, particularly if they've already booked their flights but occasionally things outside of their control do happen and they may need to cancel on you. In these situations it's good to have a Plan B.

If you'd still like to house sit, the easiest house sits to get accepted for are the last minute ones (where there's less competition and the homeowner is in desperate need of someone) and house sits where you can meet the homeowner first. If the homeowner has cancelled after you've already booked your flights, apply for house sits in that area and explain that you've already booked your flights. Many homeowners will be more considerate of you if they know that your flights are already booked.

Failing that you should try to make the best out of an unfortunate situation. The chapter on finding cheap accommodation towards the back of this book will help you find somewhere else to stay. If your original house sit is in somewhere where hotels are expensive, consider going into the countryside or to another town or city where accommodation is cheaper.

Are we too young to house sit?

Getting accepted for a house sit when you're under 30 can be hard. It's even harder if you're under 25.

Although many homeowners will decline you outright based on your age, if you build up lots of references (often the only strategy is to apply for just about every house sit until you get accepted for one) you will gradually find that with more references, homeowners are less likely to decline you based on your age.

What should I do if a house sit isn't as advertised?

Not every house sit is perfect and occasionally things will go wrong. It's important that you take as much as you can in your stride and try to make the best of a bad situation.

A common situation is that the homeowner hasn't cleaned and tidied the house for your arrival. As frustrating as this is, often it's easier to just grin and bear it and clean the place yourself.

In very rare circumstances things may go so badly wrong that the only feasible solution seems to be to leave. You should only do this if you've exhausted every other possible way of making this work including having spoken to the homeowner, explained the problems and given them time to rectify the situation.

Leaving a house sit means the homeowner will need to either cancel their vacation or ask someone else to step in to cover things until they get back or can find an alternative sitter. While you may want to just walk out, it's important to think about the welfare of the pets you're leaving behind before doing so. Again, it's important to stress that this should really be if there's no possible way to sort the situation out.

Although these kind of house sitting situations are rare, it's good to be prepared for them. The best way to be prepared is to have a house sitting agreement, where the expectations of the house sit and the responsibilities of both homeowner and house sitter are clearly laid out for both parties.

If a homeowner doesn't keep their side of the agreement, you'll have something signed by them to point to, and will find it a lot easier to convince yourself that it's okay to walk out.

House sitting for profit

Yes it's possible to house sit and get paid for it. Although this book is more concerned with house sitting in return for free accommodation, the following chapter will give you a short introduction to finding paid house sitting opportunities.

Note: Since you're getting paid to house sit, you'll need to read up on the individual laws of your country with regards to setting up a house and pet sitting business. It's also worth doing a quick Google search for pet and house sitters in your area to see what they offer. How much do they charge? Do they have insurance? Reading up about what they offer should help to give you an idea of what your business should also offer.

Once you're certain this is something that you want to do, the next step is to work out how you'll attract customers.

Create a website

First a foremost, you should create a website for your new business. Building a website is another book in itself, however these days you don't need to understand programming to make your own website. There are plenty of fairly straight-forward website builders such as Squarespace, Wix and Weebly that will satisfy the needs of anyone just looking for a simple small business website.

If you're looking for something slightly more complex and don't mind a bit of learning, WordPress is another good solution. This is the software that powers most blogs you see on the web today, as well as a large number of websites. While Squarespace, Wix and Weebly make it easy to build simple websites that require just a couple of pages of text and images, WordPress allows you to build websites with more advanced features.

List yourself on house sitting websites

While the majority of people who use sites like Trusted Housesitters and Housecarers house sit for free, there are a couple of house sitters on there that charge. There's nothing to stop you joining and saying you charge as well, although you would have to have a compelling reason as to why someone should pay you (if you have insurance for example) when there are people who will house sit for free.

Caretaker job websites

Jobs that are aimed at caretakers, as opposed to house sitters, tend to offer some form of pay and sometimes even a full-time salary. Two websites that list caretaker opportunities are Caretaker.org and thelady.

Dog boarding websites

There are an increasing number of peer-to-peer dog boarding websites, where anyone can set themselves up as a 'host' and look after other people's pets in their own home. Some sites also have the option to pet sit in other people's homes, as opposed to just hosting in your own home as well.

Sites to look at include:

- DogVacay.com

- Rover.com

- Pawshake.com

- Dogbuddy.com

Advertise on classifieds websites

Craigslist (popular in the US), Gumtree (popular in the UK and Australia) and Kijiji (popular in Canada) are all good places to advertise your new house sitting business, either for free or relatively inexpensively.

Other Useful Travel Tips

Finding cheap flights

Accommodation and flights are two of the most expensive aspects of travelling. House sitting cuts down on the cost of accommodation, but as great as that is, there's still the cost of flights to consider.

It's worth doing some research on air miles credit cards (cards that reward you with free flights for spending with them), particularly if you live in the US where these types of credit cards are most commonly available. There are thousands of websites and forums dedicated to discussing which credit cards offer the best deals and they go into this in far more depth than this book ever could. In short the concept revolves around signing up for the credit card with the best deal, using that card for all of your purchases and then paying it off in full so you don't accumulate any charges. Unfortunately air miles credit cards aren't as prevalent in a lot of the rest of the world and so if you don't live in the US, you'll have to be more research-focused to cut down on the cost of flights.

The first step to finding cheap flights is to use a flight comparison search engine instead of going direct to the airline's webpage. Kayak is probably the biggest of these but it's also worth knowing about Skyscanner and Momondo as well. Both compare flights worldwide but are particularly good at comparing flights within Europe. Skyscanner also allows you to search for the best options across a whole month or year which is very useful for finding the best time to fly to a country you're interested in visiting. Google has also joined the game of flight search with Google.com/flights.

If you're planning on doing a multi-city or around-the-world-flight it may be worth enlisting the help of a Flight Fox. Flightfox.com is a community of flight search experts who will take your trip details and find you the best price. It isn't free to use but you only pay if they're able to beat the price you've found.

Other cheap travel accommodation

Even if you're lucky enough to line up several house sits back-to-back, there will always be a few gaps in between, even if it's just for a night or two each side.

In these instances, and in case a house sit ever falls through and you need a Plan B, it's good to know about some of the cheap accommodation options that there are out there.

The following options start with the cheapest and work their way up.

Couchsurfing & hospitality exchanges

Stay with someone else, usually on their couch. It's free and a good way to travel cheaply and make friends but it's not suited to those that like having their own personal space.

Popular sites include:

- Couchsurfing.com

- Hospitality Club

- Global Freeloaders

- Stay4free

- BeWelcome.org

WWOOFing & work exchanges

Work on an organic farm in exchange for your board. These days WWOOF isn't the only organization that facilitates work exchanges and so you can find other opportunities other than farm work. Any work that involves animal care may also be a relevant reference for your house sitting profile.

Popular sites include:

- WWOOF

- Helpx

- Workaway

Camping

Some house sitters like to camp in between house sits. Carrying a tent can be tricky but if you're a fan of the great outdoors and cheap living, camping is an accommodation alternative to consider.

Stay in a monastery (Italy)

In Italy it's possible to rent a room in a monastery. The rooms are usually very basically furnished and lack most if any of the mod cons you'd find in a hotel. That's part of the experience of course and it's an experience to try at least once.

More information about monastery stays can be found at: www.monasterystays.com

Hostels

Hostels often get a bad rap for attracting a younger, party-loving crowd however not all hostels are the same. An increasing number are trying to mimic boutique hotels on a cheaper scale while the YHA Hostels and Hostelling International Hostels tend to be well-suited to mature travelers.

To find hostels visit either HostelBookers or HostelWorld. Booking.com also features a number of hostels on their website.

Hotels

For finding cheap hotels, hotelscombined.com is easily the best website. It compares several different hotels websites and shows you the different deals and hotels from each.

If there isn't a price difference, often it makes sense to book through Hotels.com as Hotels.com has a loyalty program which allows you to earn free nights.

Several hotel websites such as Hotels.com are members of cashback websites such as TopCashback (topcashback.com in the USA and topcashback.co.uk in the UK). These sites pass the commission they typically earn for sending visitors to a website back to the consumer so it's possible to save around 10% on each stay by using a cashback site.

Apartment rentals

Short-term apartment rentals are often about the same price as a budget hotel and typically provide you with a lot more space and home comforts than a hotel normally would. A number of sites, such as Airbnb, also allow the hosts to set discounted monthly rates so it can be a good option for stays of a couple of weeks or even months as well.

Some of the main websites for apartment rentals are:

- Airbnb

- Housetrip

- Wimdu

- Roomorama

- VRBO

- 9Flats

The End

Thank you for taking the time to read through The Complete Guide to House Sitting. If you have any questions or comments, please get in touch with us through housesittingguide.com. We will be more than happy to answer any questions you have.

If you've enjoyed this book, it would also mean a lot to us if you would give this book a quick review on Amazon.com (for US & most other countries), or whichever of the following is most appropriate.

Made in the USA
Coppell, TX
15 February 2020